Climate Change

Colin Hynson

FRANKLIN WATTS
LONDON • SYDNEY

First published in 2008
by Franklin Watts

Copyright © Franklin Watts 2008

Franklin Watts
338 Euston Road
London NW1 3BH

Franklin Watts Australia
Level 17/207 Kent Street
Sydney, NSW 2000

Editor: Jeremy Smith
Design: Simon Borrough
Art director: Jonathan Hair

Picture credits: Ozgur Artug/Shutterstock: 35. Henk
Bentlage/Shutterstock: 13tl. Aleksander
Bolbot/Shutterstock: 32. Chia Yuen Che/Shutterstock:
21. Ashley Cooper/Corbis: 17tr. Creative/Getty Images:
40. Francis Dean/Rex Features: 37. Eye
Ubiquitous/Rex Features: 15. Florida Stock
/Shutterstock: 16. David Garry/Shutterstock: 29. Eric
de Graef fotografie/Shutterstock: 8. Mike
Grandmaison/ Corbis: 19. Sutton-Hibbert/
Rex Features: 22. Image Source/Rex Features: 28.
Dan Kenyon/Getty Images: 41. KPA/Zuma/Rex
Features: 25. Tiaw Leong/Shutterstock: 20. Pavel
Losevsky/Shutterstock: 13tr. Iucwa/Shutterstock: back
cover. Momatiuk - Eastcott /Corbis: front cover b.
Tatyana Morozova/Shutterstock: 17tl. NASA: 26, 38.
Vyacheslav Osokin/Shutterstock: 23. Rex Features: 14.
RIA NOVOSTI /Science Photo Library: 30. Rickey
Rogers/Reuters/Corbis: 11. Science Photo Library: 10.
John Selby/Rex Features: 34 Cliff leSergent/Alamy:
front cover t. Adrian Sherratt/Rex Features: 6. Maksim
Shmeljov/Shutterstock: 39. Shout/Rex Features: 36.
Sipa Press/Rex Features: 24. Stephen Strathdee/
erstock: 27l. Tania Zbrodko/Shutterstock: 33.

A CIP catalogue record for this book
is available from the British Library.

Dewey number: 629.47

ISBN 978 0 7496 8100 5

Printed in China

Franklin Watts is a division of
Hachette Children's Books,
an Hachette Livre UK company
www.hachettelivre.co.uk

Contents

What is global warming?

It seems that every time we open a newspaper or watch the news on the television there is a new warning about the damaging effects of a changing climate. Crop yields are down, water supplies are running low, extreme weather is becoming more common and the world's wildlife is struggling to survive.

A factory in Germany belches out fumes that contribute towards global warming.

Different words

People often use phrases like 'global warming', 'climate change' or 'the greenhouse effect'. All of these phrases mean roughly the same thing: that we are putting gases into the atmosphere and that this is changing the world's climate and weather. When people talk about global warming they mean that the temperatures around the world are gradually rising. Climate change means that the usual climates around the world are slowly changing. For example, it may mean that winters will be longer or wetter, as well as warmer. It also refers to the fact that extreme weather events, such as storms and hurricanes, are going to be more frequent. Lastly, the greenhouse effect explains the science behind climate change.

'**Greenhouse gases** are a class of gases that can trap heat near Earth's surface. As they increase in the atmosphere, the extra heat they trap leads to global warming. This warming in turn places pressure on Earth's climate system and can lead to climate change.' **Tim Flannery**, a scientist from Macquire University in Australia.

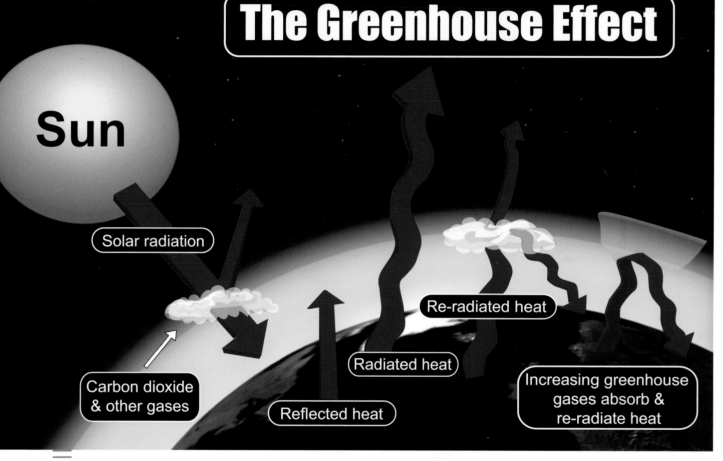

The Greenhouse Effect

Sun

Solar radiation

Carbon dioxide & other gases

Reflected heat

Radiated heat

Re-radiated heat

Increasing greenhouse gases absorb & re-radiate heat

A diagram showing how the greenhouse effect happens.

The science of global warming

The Earth is surrounded by the atmosphere, a layer of clouds and different gases. The sun's rays warm up the Earth. Some of this heat escapes back into space. However, different gases in the atmosphere, such as carbon dioxide or methane, prevent much of the heat from getting away. This natural effect keeps the Earth at a fairly constant temperature and allows life to flourish. When the amount of these 'greenhouse gases' remains constant then the temperature on Earth remains steady. However, if the amount of these gases increases then more heat will be trapped and the Earth will start to warm up.

The greenhouse planet

The planet Venus is in many ways like our own, being roughly the same size and mass. However, Venus' atmosphere is very different to Earth's and is over 95 per cent carbon dioxide. This means that virtually none of the heat caused by the Sun's rays can escape, allowing temperatures on Venus to reach over 460°C. This is much hotter than temperatures on Earth or even on Mercury, even though Mercury is much closer to the Sun.

The discovery of global warming

Scientific warnings about the effects of global warming on the planet only began to be heard in the 1980s. Before this the science was not advanced enough for any accurate predications to be made. However, the science that would explain global warming began at the start of the 19th century.

Early discoveries

It was the French scientist, Jean Fourier, who first looked at how the atmosphere could affect the world's temperature. In 1824 he suggested that gases in the atmosphere might help to explain why the temperature of the Earth was constant. He thought that this happened because some of the Sun's heat was retained by the atmosphere. Sixty years later a Swedish scientist called Svante Arrhenius was researching the causes of ice ages. He was the first to propose that it was carbon dioxide that affected the Earth's temperature. He was also the first to say that increased carbon dioxide levels from human activity may make the world warmer.

The French scientist, Jean Fourier.

XVIII Cúpula do Grupo do R
Rio de Janeiro - Br**** - 2004

A lone voice

By the 1930s, scientists around the world had begun to notice that, since the start of the century, temperatures in North America and Europe had been rising. However, it was believed that this was just a natural change in temperature and was not happening all over the world. An English engineer, Guy Stewart Callendar, disagreed. He believed that rises in the Earth's temperature were worldwide and were due to people burning fossil fuels and so releasing carbon dioxide into the atmosphere.

The world acts

By the early 1960s, scientists had proved that the amount of carbon dioxide in the atmosphere was increasing. It took another 30 years for the world to really begin to take notice. In 1992, the United Nations Earth Summit met at Rio de Janeiro in Brazil. Over 172 governments took part in this crucial meeting, with 108 of them sending their head of government. For the first time in history, the world starting to make a commitment to reducing greenhouse gases.

THOUGHT BOX

It took about 30 years for the world's leaders to start to act on the scientific proof of climate change. What do you think caused this delay?

'In my life **I have dreamt** of seeing great herds of wild animals, jungles and rainforests full of birds and butterflies. But now I wonder if they will even exist for my children to see. Did you have to worry about these things when you were young?'
Severn Suzuki, a 13-year-old Canadian speaking at the Earth Summit

11

What is causing global warming?

The science of global warming is not a simple one. However, it is generally agreed that certain gases are the cause. Research continues into where these gases are coming from and how to combat them.

The greenhouse gases

From the start carbon dioxide was seen as the main greenhouse gas and it continues to be the main problem, responsible for 60 per cent of the greenhouse effect. Methane and nitrous oxide are also greenhouse gases. Other greenhouse gases are the naturally occurring water vapour and ozone, as well as the man-made chlorofluorocarbons.

Where is the carbon dioxide coming from?

Carbon dioxide is mainly released by burning fossil fuels in power stations and factories, as well as in engines to power forms of transport including cars, ships and aircraft and heating or

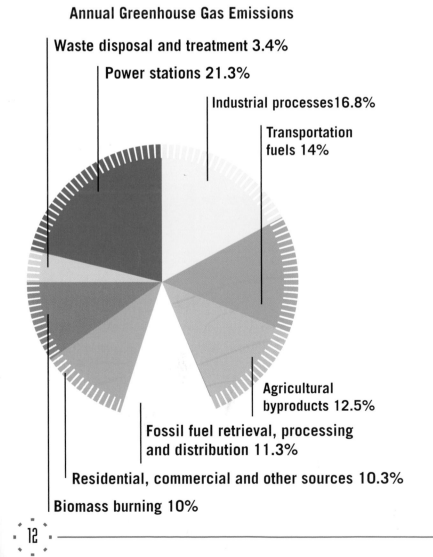

Annual Greenhouse Gas Emissions

Waste disposal and treatment 3.4%

Power stations 21.3%

Industrial processes16.8%

Transportation fuels 14%

Agricultural byproducts 12.5%

Fossil fuel retrieval, processing and distribution 11.3%

Residential, commercial and other sources 10.3%

Biomass burning 10%

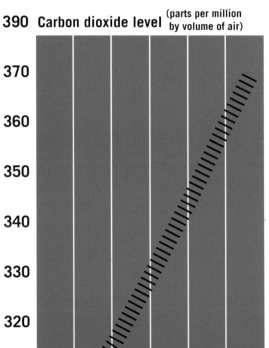

Atmospheric Carbon Dioxide

390 Carbon dioxide level (parts per million by volume of air)

370

360

350

340

330

320

310

1960 1970 1980 1990 2000

Above: Methane released by animals such as cows is a major contributor to global warming.

Above right: When petrol is burnt, carbon dioxide is released into the atmosphere.

air-conditioning systems. When forests are cut down and trees are burnt, carbon dioxide is released. We also lose the ability of these plants to convert this gas back into oxygen, as they use carbon dioxide to grow and release oxygen as a byproduct.

Sources of other greenhouse gases

The level of methane in the atmosphere is rising due to the increase in livestock farming worldwide; grazing animals produce methane when they are digesting grass. Rice growing, landfill sites, mining and drilling also release some methane. The use of nitrogen-based fertilisers releases nitrous

oxide into the atmosphere while chlorofluorocarbons were used in spray cans, cleaning products and refrigerators but their use is now controlled.

How should greenhouse gases be measured?

There is some debate about the best way to measure how much carbon dioxide is produced by each country. The simplest way is to look at the total amount of this gas produced by each country. Using this method, the United States produces the most carbon dioxide followed by China, Russia, India and Japan. However, some countries, such as China and India, argue that we should divide the amount of carbon dioxide created by the number of people in each country. Using this method, the United States is the 14th most polluting country and China and India are not even in the top thirty. The tiny and very wealthy country of Qatar produces the most carbon dioxide per head of population.

'It must be pointed out that **climate change** has been caused by the long-term historic emissions of developed countries and their high per capita emissions. '
Jiang Yu, spokesman from the Foreign Ministry of China

13

Changing weather

As the planet warms up one of the most noticeable effects on all of us will be climate change all over the world. This will not only make weather all over the world warmer but will change other kinds of weather too. Different parts of the world will become wetter in the winter and drier in the summer. Extreme weather events, such as hurricanes and storms, will become more common.

A chart showing the variations (ºc) from the average air temperature over the last 150 years. Twelve of the thirteen warmest years in history occured between 1995-2007.

0.6
0.4
0.2
0.0
-0.2
-0.4
-0.6

1860 1880 1900 1920 1940 1960 1980 2000

Extreme weather

2007 was the eighth warmest year ever recorded. It was beaten by 1998, 2005, 2003, 2002, 2004, 2006 and 2001. Since the start of the 21st century, only the year 2000 did not enter the record books. Various parts of the world are now facing extremely hot summers. These create water shortages, crop failures and deaths from heat stroke. There are also many more forest fires in both Europe and North America. In addition, in 2005, North America suffered three of the six most powerful hurricanes ever recorded – hurricanes Wilma, Rita and Katrina. In 2000, Japan recorded the heaviest rainfall in over 100 years, while Israel experienced the heaviest snowfall in 50 years.

In 2005, Hurricane Katrina caused devestation in New Orleans, USA.

'I think we have a lot to worry about. **Cyclones** and tropical storms have been getting much worse since the 1980s. We had a big **drought** starting in 1999. **Flooding** from extreme high tides is increasing also. In the late 1990s, water started coming out of the ground – first puddles, then a whole sea. That had nothing to do with rain.'

Hilia Vavae, a meteorologist from Tuvalu, speaking in 2004

Rising seas

As temperatures around the world rise then the ice at the Arctic and the Antarctic is beginning to melt. This adds fresh water to the world's oceans. Although it is predicted that the oceans will only rise by a few centimetres, this is enough to create problems all over the world. Many small countries in the Pacific and Indian Oceans, such as Tuvalu and the Maldives, could disappear under the waves. Low-lying countries, such as Bangladesh, will also suffer from increased flooding. Equally, low-lying cities including London, Lagos and New York, will become more vulnerable to flooding.

Australian drought

Australia is currently enduring its worst drought in over 100 years. The drought started in 2003 in many parts of the country and is still continuing today. Australia is also experiencing record summer temperatures. Many people in Australian towns have had to cope with water rationing and it has had a terrible effect on farmers and their crops.

Farmers in countries such as Australia have found their crops badly affected by the lack of rainfall caused by global warming.

The natural world

As the weather around the world begins to change it will start to have an effect on all living things. Many plants and animals depend on the seasons arriving at a particular time and on the weather remaining more or less the same during those seasons. Climate change around the world means that many plants and animals are under threat.

Getting warmer

Areas of the world that are generally cold, such as mountain regions in Europe and North America and the Antarctic, are getting warmer. This is beginning to have an impact on the wildlife in the area. It has been estimated that by 2080, up to 60 per cent of all plants and animals will become extinct in mountain areas. In the Antarctic and Arctic, melting ice is making life far more difficult for animals such as polar bears, penguins and arctic geese, as the animals and plants they feed off decrease in number.

'You don't have to be a polar scientist to see that if you take away all the sea ice, you don't have polar bears any more.' **Dr Andrew Derocher**, University of Alberta

Coral reefs are one of the environments most under threat by global warming.

Exit Glacier, like many Alaskan glaciers has retreated massively in the last few years due to global warming.

Under the sea

Coral reefs are home to a quarter of all marine life, making them one of the richest habitats worldwide. Reefs, such as the Great Barrier Reef off the coast of Australia, depend on the sea temperature remaining constant. As the seas begin to warm up then the coral reefs will start to die. This will have a huge impact on the fish and other animals that depend on the coral reefs for their survival. A rise in sea temperatures elsewhere is also hitting fish populations and other animals such as sea turtles.

Moving and staying

Animals and plants have reacted to climate change by moving to areas where the temperatures are more to their liking. During the late 1990s, a study tracked 14 European butterflies. They found that 9 of them have moved 193 kilometres further north. In Britain, over 20 bird species are nesting several weeks earlier than they used to. Slowly Canadian trees and small animals move northwards as temperatures begin to climb. Animals and plants that are already in these areas will find themselves in competition with these newcomers for food and shelter.

THOUGHT BOX

Different species around the world are threatened with extinction because of climate change. Do you think that we should try and save them or allow them to disappear? Why?

Agriculture, food and water

A farmer crosses his bone-dry and cracked paddy field in Boyolali, Indonesia.

One of the ways in which climate change will have an impact on all of us will be the way it will alter our food and water supplies. Even with advances in agricultural technology, crops rely on water and heat in order to grow. If there is too little or too much of either of them then there will be an impact on crops around the world.

Too little water

As droughts begin to become more common around the world then more crops will begin to fail. This will mean that there is less food to feed a growing world population. Areas such as Africa are already experiencing losses in their maize crops because of drought conditions. It is believed that deserts, such as the Kalahari, will spread into farmland of South Africa, Botswana, Angola and Zimbabwe. Wheat yields in Europe and North America are also falling and this has meant higher prices for food such as bread.

Too much water

Rising sea levels mean that severe flooding around the world will become more common. Crops in low-lying countries, such as Bangladesh, are being destroyed by increased flooding. More floods and higher rainfall will also wash away soil from farmland. This will make land far less fertile and will mean less growth.

Increasing crops

In the next few decades climate change may actually increase crop yields in some parts of the world. In cooler regions crops will benefit from a slight rise in temperature. Regions that were previously covered with ice might be turned into farmland. Plants also rely on carbon dioxide for growth, so if there is more carbon dioxide in the atmosphere then plants will grow stronger. It will be the wealthier parts of the world – North America and Europe – that will benefit from these increased crop yields.

THOUGHT BOX

If crop yields in wealthy nations grow while poorer countries produce less food, then should the wealthy nations give some of their food to those countries that are suffering?

'Africa is our greatest worry.

Many countries are already in difficulties ... and we see a pattern emerging. Southern Africa is definitely becoming drier and everyone agrees that the climate there is changing. We would expect areas which are already prone to drought to become drier with climate change.'

Wulf Killman, United Nations Food and Agriculture Organisation, 2005

Farmers in areas with cooler climates such as Canada may experience increased crop yields as a result of global warming.

Rich and poor

Climate change will eventually influence every single person on the planet. However, it will hit some people harder than others. Poor, developing countries in Africa and Asia will bear the brunt of global warming whilst wealthier, developed countries will be better able to defend themselves against the worst effects. The fact that it is these wealthy nations that have created most of the greenhouse gases makes this even harder for developing countries to bear.

Creating greenhouse gases

However you measure greenhouse gas emissions, it is the richer countries in the developed world that are putting the most greenhouse gases into the atmosphere. Europe and the United States together account for over 30 per cent of greenhouse gas emissions. African nations contribute very little. The African country that creates the most greenhouse gases is South Africa and it accounts for just 1.6 per cent of emissions. Nearly every other country in Africa contributes less than 0.5 per cent to the world total.

The human impact

All of the changes in the weather that will happen as a result of global warming will hit developing countries hardest. Increased droughts in Africa and Asia will mean that crops will fail. Flooding due to rising sea levels will be much more of a problem in countries such as Bangladesh, the Pacific Islands and African cities close to the sea, such as Lagos in Nigeria and Alexandria in Egypt. Developed countries will also suffer the effects of global warming but they will have the money to do something about it. For instance, although London is threatened by rising sea levels, very expensive flood defences are being planned.

Low lying cities, such as Alexandria in Egypt, will be threatened by rising sea levels.

'Kericho is a high altitude area and the cold weather used to ensure that mosquitoes could not survive here. However, one of the effects of the higher temperatures is the increased number of mosquitoes resulting in increased incidence of malaria in this district. This started in the 1980s. Now, people are even dying from malaria, something that was virtually unheard of 20-30 years ago.'

Nelly Damaris Chepkoskei, a farmer in Kenya, 2008

Increased disease

Of all living things, insects may actually benefit from climate change. Insects have been found in areas where they had not previously been recorded. If there are more insects then attacks on crops are more likely. However, it is the spread of one type of insect that is causing the most concern. Mosquitoes and the diseases they bring, such as malaria and dengue fever, are starting to spread across Africa and South America. It is likely that some of these diseases will appear in Europe and North America, but better health systems mean that it will be much less of a problem.

Insects such as the mosquito have thrived in the warmer temperatures brought about by global warming. Mosquitoes like this one carry the disease malaria, spreading it by biting. Its increase has meant a massive rise in the number of people dying from malaria and other diseases.

The UN Earth Summit and Kyoto

止！京都議定書発効

KYOTO: NEW DAWN FOR THE CLIMAT

GREENPEACE

A Maiko girl from Kyoto stands in front of a Greenpeace sign marking the implementation of the Kyoto Protocol Agreement.

Climate change is a problem for the whole world. Because the problem is worldwide then the solution should also involve all of the countries of the world. Every country will need to make some sacrifices and international co-operation is needed to make sure that those sacrifices are fairly shared out.

'It might take another 30 Kyotos over the next century to cut global warming down to size.'

Jerry Mahlman, director of the Geophysical Fluid Dynamics Laboratory at Princeton University

The Earth Summit

As a response to the growing concern about global warming, in 1989 the United Nations created the Intergovernmental Panel on Climate Change (IPCC). The task of this panel was to bring together all of the research being done into climate change and to produce reports. The first report was published in 1990. Their findings led to the UN Earth Summit at Rio de Janeiro in Brazil in 1992, attended by over 100 heads of government. At the end of the summit, 154 countries signed the United Nations Framework Convention on Climate Change (UNFCCC). However, the UNFCCC only committed governments to a voluntary aim of slowing down the growth of greenhouse gas emissions.

Arriving at Kyoto

The governments that signed up to the UNFCCC agreed to meet every year to look at what progress was being made. It soon became clear that the voluntary agreements in the UNFCCC were not working. Many governments were unwilling to slow down their greenhouse gas emissions. A compulsory agreement was needed and at the end of 1997 the IPCC met at Kyoto in Japan to agree on greenhouse gas reductions.

Agreements at Kyoto

At the end of the Kyoto meeting governments around the world committed themselves to reducing the amount of greenhouse gases that they produced. The wealthiest nations were required to cut their emissions whilst poorer nations had no obligations apart from monitoring their greenhouse gas emissions. It was then left up to each government to sign the international agreement. In order for the Kyoto agreement to come into force it needed to be ratified – approved – by a certain number of governments. Many countries signed up to the Kyoto Protocol quickly whilst others were more reluctant because they were afraid that it would damage their economies.

A chimney belches out smoke in northern China.

THOUGHT BOX

The voluntary agreement at Rio's Earth Summit was seen as not working properly. Why do you think that governments were reluctant to meet their voluntary targets?

The Kyoto Protocol

The Kyoto Protocol was the first real attempt to commit governments around the world to cut greenhouse gas emissions. However, getting enough governments to approve the Protocol was not easy and there were moments when it seemed that the whole process would collapse.

Europe and Kyoto

On May 31st 2002, all 15 members of the European Union ratified the Kyoto Protocol. It was agreed that the European Union as a whole would reduce their emissions by 8 per cent by 2012. However, that figure was then divided up country-by-country. This allowed some countries, such as Portugal and Luxembourg, to actually increase their greenhouse gas emissions whilst countries such as Germany and Britain have to make large cuts.

Australia and the Protocol

Despite its wealth, Australia was opposed to ratifying the Kyoto Protocol. Even though Australia was actually allowed to increase its greenhouse gas emissions by 8% under the agreement, Prime Minister John Howard refused to ratify the Protocol. He believed that it would affect Australia's economy and result in Australians losing their jobs. However, in November 2007, a general election in Australia brought in a new government and a new prime minister, Kevin Rudd, who signed the Protocol immediately.

'The world's second-largest emitter of greenhouse gases is the **People's Republic of China**. Yet, China was entirely exempted from the requirements of the Kyoto Protocol. India and Germany are among the top emitters. Yet, India was also exempt from Kyoto.' **President George W Bush (above)**, 2006

United States opposition and assent

Opposition to the Protocol in the United States under President George W Bush continued. His main objections were that it would damage the American economy and that China, the second largest emitter of greenhouse gases, is not obliged to make any cuts in emissions. Even though the US government has refused to ratify the Protocol, several US states have agreed to meet the 7 per cent reduction that the United States was supposed to reach. These include New York, Maryland, California and Delaware. Over 740 American cities have also agreed to a 7 per cent cut.

The Protocol becomes legal

After Russia ratified the Protocol in 2004, bringing the total number of countries to 141, the Kyoto Protocol became legal. Since then, others countries have ratified the agreement, notably Australia in 2007, sometimes after pressure from other governments.

THOUGHT BOX

Do you think that some poorer countries such as India and China should be exempted from cutting their greenhouse gases even though they both produce large amounts of these gases?

THOUGHT BOX

The film star and politician Arnold Schwarzenegger (below) once said about the climate change sceptics, "If you have a sick child and 98 doctors say she needs medication and two say she does not, I go with the 98 doctors." Are the sceptics wrong just because they are in a minority?

Doubters and sceptics

There is a broad agreement amongst scientists that climate change is real and that it is being caused by human activity. However, there are still some scientists who doubt the science behind climate change. Most of these scientists either believe that the science of climate change is still too uncertain or that there are natural explanations for global warming rather it being due to human activity. Here are some of their arguments.

A natural warming

The temperature of the Earth has changed rapidly several times over the past five million years, during which time there have been at least four ice ages. In the medieval period, Europe had a warmer climate between the years 1000 and 1300. After that date until about 1800, temperatures in many parts of the world fell. These natural changes in temperature have a number of causes, such as solar activity or the amount of carbon dioxide that is naturally produced. Some scientists, such as Robert Balling and Sallie Baliunas, believe that the changes in temperature that we are seeing can be explained by natural causes and are nothing to do with human activity.

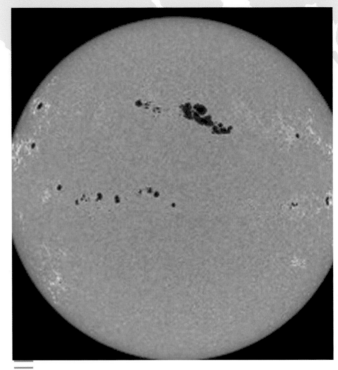

Some scientists believe that global warming is due to natural phenomena such as sunspots (above), rather than carbon emissions caused by humans.

Heat islands

It is well-known that urban areas are usually warmer than rural ones because of the heat produced by all of the buildings in towns and cities. Some global warming sceptics, including Stephen McIntyre, believe that this accounts for the high temperatures recorded recently. However, temperatures in rural areas have been shown to be rising as well.

'I am convinced that in 15-20 years, we will look back on this period of global warming hysteria as we now look back on so many other popular and trendy scientific ideas.' **William Gray**, Colorado State University, 2005

Funding the sceptics

Many climate change sceptics, such as Fred Singer and Patrick Michaels, have been criticised because they have been linked to organisations that are funded by oil companies. These organisations have been created in order to cast doubt on the science of global warming as fossil fuel companies want to be allowed to continue doing business unchecked.

The Danish academic Bjorn Lomborg.

The sceptical environmentalist

In 2007 a Danish academic called Bjorn Lomborg published a book called *Cool It! The Skeptical Environmentalist's Guide to Global Warming*. In his book he argues that while there is no doubt that global warming is happening, it is a natural phenomenon, and rather than trying to cut emissions it would be better and cost less to focus on funding research into new technologies to prevent further climate change and to improve life for the world's poorest peoples.

What can we do?
Individuals, governments and international bodies

THOUGHT BOX

Would you be ready to spend your own money on energy-saving improvements to your home? Would you do it if you knew that other people were doing nothing?

An environmental group in the USA meet to discuss strategies to cut global carbon emissions.

Most people agree that action to combat climate change is the responsibility of us all. Individuals, governments, businesses and international organisations all have a part a play. The question remains, how much responsibility should each of us take? If we are going to do something about climate change then should that be voluntary or should we be forced to do something by our governments?

Individuals and governments

Environmental groups and governments around the world are constantly calling on individuals to take action to cut down on greenhouse gases. Books, websites and television adverts give us advice on how we can help in the battle against climate change. However, this relies on individuals deciding to do this on a voluntary basis. Naturally, some people will take action but many will not. Environmental groups say that voluntary action can only be one part of the plan. Governments should also pass laws which will force people to change their lifestyles so that they produce less greenhouse gases. However, this may mean that we have less freedom of choice and any laws would have to be carefully thought out so as not to hit the poorest people the hardest.

Businesses and climate change

Because so many greenhouse gases are produced by businesses then they should also cut down on their emissions. This could actually help businesses to make money by spending less on energy. However, it would cost a lot of money at the start to invest in new machinery or buildings and many businesses are reluctant to do this unless they know that other businesses will do the same. Governments could pass laws to force businesses to produce less greenhouse gases but this might lead to more expensive goods in shops.

Governments and international bodies

The Kyoto Protocol shows that international co-operation is possible and may be the best way to cut greenhouse gases across the world. When the governments met at Kyoto, all of them went there to try and get the best deal for their country. This may not be the same as finding the best solution to climate change. Every government was concerned that cutting down on greenhouse gases may be unpopular at home. Cuts in greenhouse gases might mean that jobs will be lost or people's standard of living will go down.

Countries such as the UK can pass laws in Parliament to encourage business to invest in greener ways of working.

'Just boiling enough water needed to make a cup of tea, not leaving a mobile phone charger plugged in or turning appliances off of standby will all help to **reduce the amount of energy wasted**. If everyone took these simple actions then the amount of energy saved collectively would be substantial.' **Philip Selwood**, chief executive of the Energy Saving Trust

What can we do? Fuel efficiency

Nearly all of the machines that we use as part of our everyday lives use a lot of energy. Everything from the car in the drive to the fridge in the kitchen and the bulbs in our light sockets use energy. There are now energy-efficient cars and household goods that do the same job but use far less energy. Buying these energy-efficient goods could significantly cut greenhouse gas emissions.

These G-Wiz electric cars are totally emission free, saving between one and three tonnes of carbon dioxide emitted by a normal car every year.

Hybrid cars

One of the ways in which cars could produce less greenhouse gases is by using hybrid power. This is when a car uses more than one source of fuel to power the engine. This is usually a petrol-driven engine and an electric motor. These kinds of car are much more fuel efficient and so produce less carbon dioxide. Some cars, such as the G-Wiz, run just on electricity and do not pollute the environment at all.

Energy in the home

Heating a home can use a lot of energy because so much of the heat is lost through the roof and walls. It has been estimated that if every home in Britain were to be properly insulated then it would cut carbon dioxide emissions by about six million tonnes a year. According to the International Energy Agency (IEA), lighting accounts for nearly 20 per cent of all electricity used. So using energy-saving light bulbs would make a big difference to the reduction in greenhouse gases.

Biofuels

Biofuels, such as ethanol and bio-diesel, are fuels that are made from crops – usually corn, rapeseed and soya beans. Although these fuels will produce greenhouse gases when they are used, the biofuel crops will absorb carbon dioxide as they grow. However, farming these crops and processing them into fuel creates greenhouse gases. Many of these crops will be grown in poorer countries on farmland once used to grow food crops. It also means that large areas of forest will be cleared to grow the crops, and deforestation adds greenhouse gases to the atmosphere.

Energy saving lightbulbs (above) use up to 80 per cent less electricity than a standard bulb, but produce the same amount of light.

Biofuels (see opposite) are a controversial way of cutting our greenhouse gas emissions. They have many benefits but serious downsides, too. Do you think that we should stop using biofuels or increase their use?

THOUGHT BOX

'Switching to biofuels would not reduce the demand for fuel, just change the way we get it. And that would require a lot of land. In fact, substituting just 10 per cent of fossil fuels to biofuels for all our vehicles would require about 40 per cent of the entire cropland in Europe and North America.' **David Suzuki**, Canadian science broadcaster, 2007

Changing our lives

Buying energy-saving light bulbs or a fuel-efficient car can help to reduce greenhouse gas emissions. Paying for your aeroplane flight to be carbon offset before taking the flight will mean that the carbon dioxide produced by that flight will be balanced out. All of these ways are useful in combating climate change. However, there are many people who believe that this is not enough and that we all have to change the way that we live our lives if any real impact is going to be made.

Children in London go to school in a 'walking bus', walking together to save energy and get fit.

Consuming less

Both governments and some environmental groups are encouraging us to buy more energy-efficient goods which produce less greenhouse gases. For other environmentalists this is not enough. They believe that if the problem of global warming is to be successfully tackled then people in wealthy countries will have to accept that the whole of their lives will have to change. This may mean sacrificing some of the comforts and conveniences that people have become used to. For instance, using a more fuel-efficient car may help to reduce carbon dioxide emissions. An even better solution would be to simply not use a car at all since walking or cycling produce no greenhouse gases. Taking the bus or train would also reduce the amount of carbon dioxide reaching the atmosphere. These alternatives do require more time and effort than using a car but it is a sacrifice that should be made.

THOUGHT BOX

Are you willing to make sacrifices in order to cut greenhouse gases? Will you give up your foreign holidays and trips in the car? If you do not want to make these changes then what effect will this have on others?

'This means the end of distant foreign holidays, unless you are prepared to take a long time getting there. It means that business meetings must take place over the Internet or by means of video conferences. It means that transcontinental journeys must be made by train or coach.

It means that journeys around the world must be reserved for visiting the people you love, and that they will require both slow travel and the saving up of carbon rations.' **George Monbiot**, Environmental campaigner, 2006

Flying abroad on holiday is a major source of carbon dioxide emissions. We may have to take our holidays at home if we wish to reduce global warming in the future.

Flying less

Air travel is the world's fastest growing source of greenhouse gases and it is growing fast. It is expected that the number of people taking flights will double in the next 15 years. This will mean larger airports, more flights from those airports and even more carbon dioxide being produced. The engines on aircraft are becoming more fuel-efficient but this will not be enough to compensate for the growth in aircraft usage. Environmentalists believe that all of us should be flying much less. This could be done voluntarily but it has also been suggested that air flights should be made much more expensive to stop people from flying round the world. Critics of this idea say that this will not stop richer people from flying but it will prevent those with less money from having that choice.

Repairing the ozone hole

It is possible for the governments of the world to get together and to agree on an effective course of action to solve an environmental problem. In the 1980s, one of the most pressing environmental problems was a hole in the atmosphere that was appearing over Antarctica at the North Pole. Public pressure and the findings of scientists forced governments around the world to find a solution to what is called the 'ozone hole'. The same international action is now required to combat global warming.

The ozone layer

About 16 kilometres up in the atmosphere is a layer of gas called ozone, a type of oxygen. The ozone layer is important because it stops too many of the sun's harmful rays getting through to Earth. These ultraviolet (UV) rays can cause skin cancer and could harm plants and animals. Life on our planet could not exist without the ozone layer.

This is a NASA photograph of the Earth, showing the ozone hole. The blue and purple colours show where there is the least amount of ozone.

'More than anything, the example set by the Montreal Protocol clearly shows that **international cooperation** among all stakeholders...can lead to rapid progress toward protection of the global environment.'
Mack McFarland, Atmospheric Scientist, 2007

Chemicals used in aerosols are partly responsible for the hole in the ozone layer.

Finding a hole

In 1986, scientists with the British Antarctic Survey discovered that there was a large hole in the ozone layer over the North Pole. Further work by scientists showed that the hole was getting bigger every year and the ozone layer was becoming thinner all over the atmosphere. It was discovered that the hole in the ozone layer was caused by chemicals called chlorofluorocarbons (CFCs). CFCs were used in most aerosol cans, refrigerators and in fire extinguishers from the 1920s onwards.

Fixing the hole

In 1987, representatives from over 190 governments met at Montreal in Canada in order to find a solution to the growing ozone hole. At the end of the meeting a treaty was signed, the Montreal Protocol, that obliged every country to phase out their use of CFCs. Poorer countries were also promised financial help to cut their CFC use. The treaty was a great success. CFCs are no longer produced in Europe and North America and will not be produced anywhere in the world by 2010. The hole above the ozone layer is beginning to close and it is believed that it will be fully closed by 2050.

Two futures

We have reached a point when all of us have to make a choice. Many of the scientists who are studying global warming are saying that we have very little time to do anything. If action is not taken very soon then it will be too late. Temperatures around the world will continue to climb and it will be unstoppable. However, there is still time. If everybody agrees to take action then the worst effects of global warming may be stopped. There are two possible futures in front of us.

Imagining the worst

In October 2003, the United States Department of Defense published a report which looked at what might happen around the world if climate change was not tackled effectively. The report was called 'Imagining the Unthinkable'. According to the report, by 2020 rising temperatures, rising sea levels and greater rainfall will mean that the United States, Europe and parts of South America will experience both more floods and more droughts. Coastal regions around the world will begin to be reclaimed by the sea forcing large numbers of people to become refugees. Water shortages and crop failures in Africa and Asia will also mean that people will try to leave their homes and make their way to Europe and North America in search of a better life. The report also imagines wars in Asia and even between the United States and China as countries struggle to control food and water for their populations.

'While the US itself will be relatively better off ... it will find itself in a world where Europe will be struggling internally, large number of refugees washing up on its shores and Asia in serious crisis over food and water.'
'Imagining the Unthinkable', US Department of Defense report, 2003

The authors of 'Imagining the Unthinkable' might be wrong. Climate change will certainly make life more difficult for many people but it may not be as bad as the report states. Is it better for us to imagine the worst before deciding what action to take?

Left: We may all have to make adjustments to our lifestyles in the future in order to stop global warming getting worse.

Growing our own food rather than importing it from far away countries will help make for a greener future.

A better future

The authors of the US Department of Defense report made it clear that what they are predicting for the next 10 to 20 years may not happen. However, if we are going to make sure that this is the case, our future lives will have to change. In this future cars and aircraft will only be used when it is really essential and all carbon dioxide created will always be offset. The amount of energy used in people's homes, schools and workplaces will be much smaller than today and most of that energy will not come from fossil fuels. People will also eat locally-produced food rather than food transported vast distances around the world.

Glossary

Atmosphere The layer of gases that surrounds the Earth. It is mostly made up of nitrogen and oxygen. Carbon dioxide is less that 0.5 per cent of the atmosphere.

Biofuels Fuels that comes from living plants that are grown and harvested for that reason.

Carbon dioxide A gas that is produced by all living things when they breathe. It is also a waste product from fossil fuels.

Developed country Countries that have industrialised, with a high standard of living.

Developing country Countries that are less industrialised, with a lower standard of living.

Drought An extended period of time when a particular region or country has gone without rain.

Fossil fuel Coal, oil and gas.

Global warming Term used to describe how the Earth will get warmer as more heat is trapped by the atmosphere.

Greenhouse effect The greenhouse effect is a way of describing the science behind climate change. It got its name because the science is similar to a glass greenhouse that lets heat in but does not allow all of it to escape.

Greenhouse gases Carbon dioxide, methane and nitrous oxide.

Heat Islands Because of the waste heat produced by built-up areas and by the cars and buses in those areas then that area is usually warmer than the surrounding countryside. These are called 'Heat Islands' and have been used by global warming sceptics to help prove their case.

Malaria An infectious disease caused by a parasite that is transmitted by the bite of an infected mosquito. Persons suffering from malaria experience periodic episodes of chills and fever.

Nuclear energy This is power produced by splitting atoms to produce a huge amount of heat. It can be used to generate electricity.

Per Capita Term meaning 'for each head'.

Protocol An international agreement.

Radiated heat Heat emitted as invisible light.

Renewable energy Energy that comes from a source that will never run out. The main forms come from the Sun, wind, tides and waves.

United Nations Global association of governments that cooperate in matters of international law, security, economic development and social equity.

Weblinks

www.foe.co.uk/campaigns/climate/issues/climate_change
The campaigning organisation, Friends of the Earth, has produced an excellent introduction to the problem of climate change.

http://epa.gov/climatechange/kids/index.html
The Environmental Protection Agency is a government agency from the United States. This is a website for young people about climate change.

http://education.arm.gov/
The ARM is part of the United States Department of Energy. This website has lots of games, quizzes, teachers' notes and lots of information on climate change.

www.ipcc.ch/index.htm
The Intergovernmental Panel on Climate Change (IPCC) created the Kyoto Protocol and is the main international forum for finding a solution to climate change. Their website contains a huge amount of information about their work.

http://science.nationalgeographic.com/science/environment/global-warming/gw-impacts-interactive.html
This website from National Geographic shows the effect that climate change will have around the world.

www.metoffice.gov.uk/education/primary/climate_change_KS2.html
The Metrological Office in the United Kingdom is one of the main centres of climate change research. This part of their website has materials on climate change for young people.

www.carbonfootprint.com/calculator.aspx
This website calculates the amount of greenhouse gases that you produce and can then advise you on to reduce your 'carbon footprint'.

www.direct.gov.uk/en/Environmentandgreenerliving/Thewiderenvironment/Climatechange/index.htm
The United Kingdom government has created a website to explain climate change and how everybody can help to tackle it.

Note to parents and teachers:
Every effort has been made by the Publishers to ensure that these websites are suitable for children, that they are of the highest educational value, and that they contain no inappropriate or offensive material. However, because of the nature of the Internet, it is impossible to guarantee that the contents of these sites will not be altered. We strongly advise that Internet access is supervised by a responsible adult.

Index